Written by Christine Lazier
Illustrated by Graham Underhill,
Pierre de Hugo, Ute Fuhr and Raoul Sautai

Specialist Adviser:
Yves Cohat
Marine Anthropologist

ISBN 0-944589-39-1
First U.S. Publication 1991 by
Young Discovery Library
217 Main St. • Ossining, NY 10562

YOUNG DISCOVERY LIBRARY

Seashore
Life

YOUNG DISCOVERY LIBRARY

Have you been to the seashore?
It's where land meets the sea.
There are three kinds of shores:
rocky, muddy and sandy.
These steep rocks are called
cliffs. Then there is the
coast, sloping into the water.

**Rain and seaspray eat away at
the cliffs.** Waves, very slowly,
wear them down. Pieces of rock
break off and become stones. The
stones break up, becoming pebbles.
The pebbles become sand and that
is how beaches are made!
Rivers also bring sand and earth.
They turn into mud in the spaces
between the rocks.

The sea rises and falls—that is the tide!

The sun and moon pull on the Earth. This makes the oceans rise and fall about every 12 hours. Why is one tide always 50 minutes later then the one the day before? Because it takes the moon almost 25 hours to make a full turn.

All kinds of things are left on the beach by the tide: bits and pieces of seaweed, shells, starfish, driftwood...

During one day each spring
and fall, the tides are higher
than usual. This is an **equinox**,
when the sun is closest to our
Earth.
Life is not easy for plants and
animals that live on the shore.
The water covers, then uncovers
them. The waves are powerful.
The sun burns, the water is salty.

They show how far the water reached at
high tide—look back at the first page.

On the beach, the sand is made of billions of tiny pieces of quartz (a mineral) and seashells.

fine sand   ordinary sand   coarse sand   black sand

Animals and plants have a hard time making their homes on pebbly beaches—the smooth stones move with the waves.

Sand fleas are tiny shellfish that hide under the wrack, or bits of seaweed, tossed up by the sea. They move up and down the beach but never get caught by a wave!

Sand flies eat rotting seaweed.

Sand fleas can jump as far as one foot!

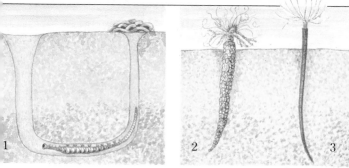

The lugworm (1), the sandmason (2) and the
sandworm (3), burrow and stay put.

At low tide the beach seems empty.
But animals live in the wet sand
and in the mud. The lugworm
swallows sand while digging its
tunnel. It takes food from the
sand then dumps it up top in a
pile. A razor clam takes less
than a minute to bury itself by
digging with its powerful foot.

The razor clam (1), cockle (2), donax (3), and clam (4), are
mollusks—they have soft bodies. Their shells are in two parts.

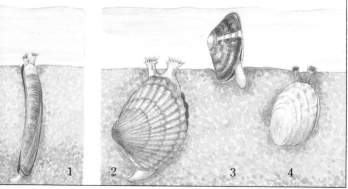

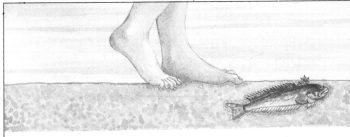

If you walk on wet sand, watch out for the sharp, poisonous spines of the sting-fish.

Farther out, where water covers the sand, there are plants called eelgrass and sea-grass. Many animals live there. The cuttlefish (1) grabs its prey with two stretchy tentacles. It can let out a black, inky cloud to confuse an enemy. Smelts (2) swim in schools. The pipefish (3) has bony plates under its skin. The dory (4) looks for mussels. The jellyfish (5) looks like an umbrella opening and closing when it moves. Crabs that swim (6) have back legs like paddles.

The flounder eats worms and little crabs.

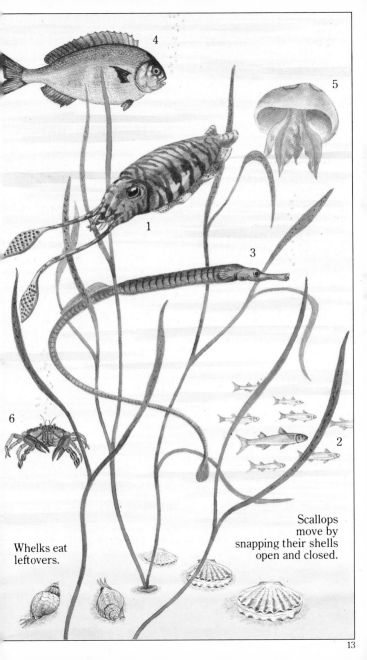

Whelks eat
leftovers.

Scallops
move by
snapping their shells
open and closed.

On warmer seashores there are seas of grass that serve as food markets.

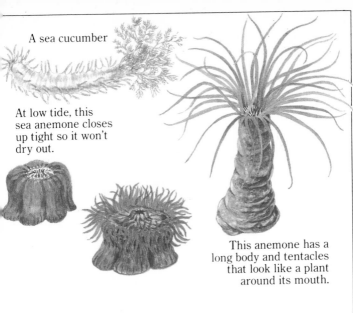

A sea cucumber

At low tide, this sea anemone closes up tight so it won't dry out.

This anemone has a long body and tentacles that look like a plant around its mouth.

This sea slug (1) lays its eggs in long ribbons that fishermen call "sea spaghetti." It is the male sea horse (2) who carries eggs in his pouch until they hatch. Bass (3) and mullet (4) swim around, looking for a meal. Watch for the stingray (5)! Its tail has poison spines. The tentacles of this jellyfish (6) can sting even after it dies.

The trepang, a type of sea cucumber, lives in the Pacific Ocean.

butterflyfish

lionfish

emperor
fish

sea
pen

The sweeping fins of the lionfish, on the left, help it to trap food.

starfish

If an arm is cut off, it can become a whole new starfish.

The long spines on its back are poisonous. Any fish who tries to eat it is making a big mistake!

Sponges attach themselves to rocks. Their soft skeletons are what you may use in your bath.

In the tropics, coral reefs are found offshore. They are made of little animals called polyps, who catch food with their tentacles. They produce a liquid that hardens into the coral.

Beautiful red coral like this is disappearing, because so much of it is taken by divers. When it is alive you can see the clear polyps sticking out.

How are dunes formed?

When the coastline is flat and open, the wind pushes the sand into piles. Dunes can reach 30 feet in height.

This is a dune on the Florida coast. The wind keeps bringing sand. The dune gets bigger and moves slowly inland.

Plants growing on dunes must live with salt, sand and little fresh water. A blue thistle's roots may go down 10 feet. Other plants have roots that spread to keep the sand down. The bindweed, a low creeper, doesn't mind gusts of wind. Everlasting flowers form a beautiful carpet.

Plants like sea purslane grow very well, even in a salty area.

1. dune slack
2. beach grass
3. bindweed
4. blue thistle
5. everlasting flower
6. aster
7. spurge

Cliffs are home to many kinds of seabirds.

In the springtime, thousands of birds mate. You can hear the noisy cries of the adults and the cheeping of the chicks. The kittiwake's nest is very sturdy. She makes it by trampling down mud, seaweed, plants and droppings. The puffin digs with its beak to make a burrow. Murres like to greet and peck at each other. Like razorbills, they are skillful undersea fishermen, coming on land only to mate and raise their young.

The fulmar glides over the water.

5

1. kittiwake
2. puffin
3. common murre
4. razorbill
5. cormorant
6. gannet

At a rocky shore

The cliffs are edged by rocks
covered with shells and seaweed.
Birds come here for their
daily food.
The oystercatcher rests here,
facing the wind. His beak
is good for digging up
lugworms, crabs and
cockles. He breaks
the shells with
his beak and gulps
down the flesh.

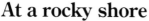

In spite of its name, the oystercatcher eats many kinds of shellfish.

One oystercatcher can eat
600 cockles in a day!
Plovers hop from rock
to rock or fly very
fast over the water.
They are always moving!
They turn over wrack and
pebbles with their strong
beaks, looking for mollusks,
shellfish or insects
hiding underneath.

The plover can
move rocks as
heavy as itself!

**When waves break over
the rocks, animals have
to hold on tightly!**
The foot of a limpet works like
a suction cup. It glides over
the rocks, nibbling seaweed.
Barnacles don't budge.
In calmer water there
are lichens, rockweed
and bladderwrack.

bladderwrack   barnacle   mussels
covered with
barnacles   abalone

yellow lichen

black lichen

rockweed

rock winkle

The mussel anchors itself with byssus,
a fine silky string produced by a gland
in its foot. To move, it glues more
strings on one side and cuts the others.

blue
periwinkle

chiton

limpet

snail

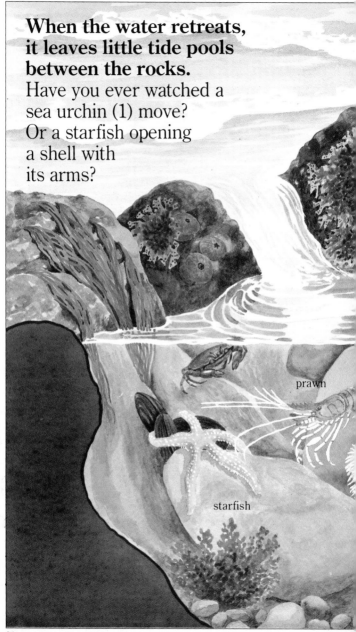

**When the water retreats,
it leaves little tide pools
between the rocks.**
Have you ever watched a
sea urchin (1) move?
Or a starfish opening
a shell with
its arms?

prawn

starfish

This crab is doing the "crab walk," of course. The hermit crab (2) borrows an empty shell to protect its soft body.

What is seaweed?...

a kind of water plant that
has no flowers or roots. Its
stems and leaves are in one
piece, called a frond. Some
seaweed are free-floating;
others attach themselves
to rocks with a holdfast,
a kind of anchor.

Sugar kelp grows on rock
or shells that
are always
under water.

sea lettuce

rockweed or "bladderwrack"—
its bladders, or pods,
are fun to pop.

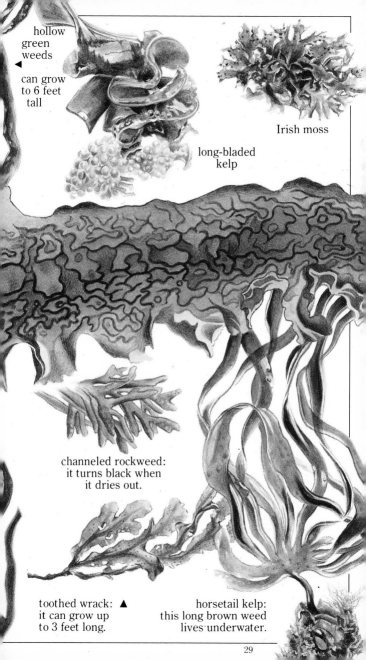

hollow green weeds ◄ can grow to 6 feet tall

Irish moss

long-bladed kelp

channeled rockweed: it turns black when it dries out.

toothed wrack: ▲ it can grow up to 3 feet long.

horsetail kelp: this long brown weed lives underwater.

The mouth of a river is called an estuary. There the muddy, fresh water of the river mixes with salty sea water. Mud settles on the bottom. Animals here have adapted to the half-fresh, half-salt water.

Oyster-farmers raise young oysters in bays. They use tiles covered with sand. The oysters attach themselves with a "glue" they produce.

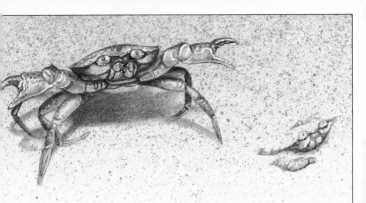

Bay crabs like muddy bottoms, but also sand and rocks. If they are in danger, they may rise up on their back legs and clack their pincers to make noise. Mostly, though, they burrow in the mud.

Some marine mammals live in estuaries: these harbor seals are lying on sand banks at low tide. Seals sometimes swim 100 miles up a river.

The sandpiper spends the winter in estuaries.

crab-eating macaque

Strange trees grow
in calm tropical waters
or in river mouths, the
mangroves. Their roots
look like stilts coming
out of the water.
You can see mangrove
swamps in Florida.

The fiddler crab has one enormous
pincer. He uses it to attract the
female into his burrow.

Monkeys and snakes live in the branches of South American mangroves. Below, crocodiles wait for prey. Macaques catch crabs at low tide.

Put on rubber boots or your beach sandals and grab a pail: **at low tide there are many things to see!**

You can collect shells and rocks of all colors, polished by the sea. You'll find hundreds in the sand.
Want to catch a razor clam? Sprinkle salt over the holes of its burrow. It will think the tide is coming in, and pop up!

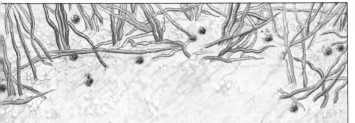

Guess which mollusks are hiding
in the sand: the razor clam, the
cockle or the surf clam?
Here's how to tell:

The razor clam
leaves two holes
close together.

The cockle's are
a little farther
apart.

The surf clam's
are wider
still.

How can you tell if limpets move?
Use nail polish to draw a circle
around their shells. Mark each
shell and circle in a different
way. At the next tide, you will
be able to
see which ones
moved.

The Tide

Sometimes we peep beneath the
    blinds,
And through the window bars.
We see the dew like silver clouds;
We see the lighted stars:

And down among the sea-weed pools
Where little fishes hide,
Swift coming through the dark we hear
The footsteps of the tide.

We know, when night is tucked away,
Tomorrow there will be
Across the flat and shining sand,
The footprints of the sea.

Marjorie Wilson

Index

Books of Discovery for children five through ten...

Young Discovery Library is an international undertaking — the series is now published in nine countries. It is the world's first pocket encyclopedia for children, 120 titles will be published.

Each title in the series is an education on the subject covered: a collaboration among the author, the illustrator, an advisory group of elementary school teachers and an academic specialist on the subject.

The goal is to respond to the endless curiosity of children, to fascinate and educate.

For a catalog of other titles,
please write to: Young Discovery,
                       P.O. Box 229,
                       Ossining, NY 10562